Guy Lawton

Spreadsheet Family Trees

Published by

David Hawgood
London
1994

Biographical details of the author

Guy Lawton retired from a senior position in the Inland Revenue in 1991, having spent the last 23 years of his career in Information Technology. Since retirement he has drawn on his computer expertise and 30 years of genealogical research to produce articles for "Family Tree Magazine" and "Family Tree Computer Magazine". He is also author of the forthcoming Public Record Office Readers' Guide "Chancery Court Proceedings for the Family Historian".

Spreadsheet Family Trees
by Guy Lawton

Copyright © Guy Lawton 1994

Published 1994 by David Hawgood,
26 Cloister Road, Acton, London W3 0DE, phone 081 993 2897,

Letters to the author can be sent via the publisher.

The family trees reproduced as Figures 3 and 8 are of the Lawton family in Cheshire; the reproductions in this book are approximately the same size as the author's original print. The centre fold (pages 16 and 17) is of the Luke family, mainly of Devon; it is reduced to A4 from the author's A3 original. The author's originals were printed on a dot matrix printer. The extract from Figure 8 on the front cover has been re-printed at a different scale on a laser printer.

The title page border is reproduced from the Dover Publications book "200 Decorative Title-Pages". It was the title page of "Four Books of Husbandry", by M Conradus Heresbachius, "Containing the whole art and trade of Husbandry, Gardening, Grafting and Planting", published in 1601.

Printed in Great Britain by Parchment (Oxford) Ltd,
Crescent Road, Cowley, Oxford OX4 2PB (phone 0865 747547).

ISBN 0 948151 10 2

CONTENTS

Page

THE BASIC SYSTEM

Drop line pedigrees	4
Spreadsheets	4
Text in spreadsheets	5
More people per page	6
Cursor movement macros	7
Family Name Macros	8
Marriage indicator macros	8
Place name macros	8
Printer control macros	9
Line drawing macros	9
Headings and cross references	10
Saving hard disk space	10
Master spreadsheet and new trees	12

ENHANCEMENTS TO THE BASIC SYSTEM

More layout details	12
Location of macros	12
Page limits	14
Title block	14
Location of menu macros	14
Menu macro of place names	15
Menu macro of double-line graphics	15
Autostart macro for initial cursor position	19
Cross references to husband's trees	19
Positioning marriage details	19

APPENDIXES

Appendix A Pedigree worksheet macros	21
Appendix B Standard layout and printer control strings	30
Appendix C Batch files	31

THE BASIC SYSTEM

Drop-line pedigrees

There are a number of ways to lay out pedigrees, and one format favoured by many genealogists is that of the traditional drop-line pedigree. This style is particularly helpful if the pedigree incorporates collateral lines, since the links between the different branches of the family are easier to present and are intuitively obvious. This factor is particularly useful when attempting to sort out relationships stated in wills in developing a pedigree. Drop-line pedigrees also facilitate the inclusion on the pedigree of ancillary information such as occupations, scholastic records, payments of taxes etc.

A method frequently recommended for preparing drop-line pedigrees on a computer is to use a word processing program. Since a word processor is designed to handle text, this seems to be the obvious tool for the job. However, word processors are not well suited to repositioning blocks of text which occupy *parts only of successive lines*. Yet such blocks of text are the essence of a pedigree.

Spreadsheets

This repositioning facility is a prime need for a pedigree under development. For instance, the later discovery of a child baptised elsewhere could require the insertion of the new child between its already incorporated siblings. In addition, fitting the pedigree on a page might require the offspring of a marriage to be split into two sections, one beneath the other. If descents from several of the existing entries had already been inserted, imagine the consequences for the layout of the insertion of the new-found child!

This paramount need for easy repositioning points to the use of a spreadsheet. Spreadsheets are primarily designed for arithmetical work. For those unfamiliar with spreadsheets, they are best visualised as the electronic equivalent of accounting paper, with columns and rows dividing the page into a number of "cells" into which figures are inserted.

For example, the columns might represent months, and the lines various items of expenditure. Such an account would not be very informative however unless month headings and row descriptions could be inserted, so spreadsheets do provide for text insertion. In addition, because their intended use frequently necessitates the insertion or deletion of columns and rows in existing layouts, spreadsheet programs provide flexible editing functions. These permit adjusting the layout without destroying the existing data, or repositioning data within an existing layout. **This is just what genealogists need!**

In order to identify particular "cells" in a spreadsheet a method similar to the use of "Eastings" and "Northings" to designate locations on Ordnance Survey maps is used. The position of a "cell" in the spreadsheet is given by quoting its column *letter* followed by its row *number*. The base or home cell is the one in the top left-hand corner of the worksheet, referred to as cell A1. It is to this cell that the "Home" key moves the cursor from anywhere in the worksheet.

The spreadsheet program automatically names the rows and columns as follows. The rows are numbered in ascending order sequentially *down* the worksheet, while the columns are lettered sequentially from *left to right* in alphabetical order. Column Z is followed by columns AA, AB, AC etc through to AY, AZ. The pattern is then repeated, with successive following columns being lettered BA, BB, BC ... BY, BZ, CA, CB ... CZ, DA, DB and so on. The program permanently displays the column letters at the top of the screen and the row numbers (in a fixed 4-character column) down the left hand side of the screen. Figure 1 helps to make this clear, and shows that cell AB4 contains the letters "pq".

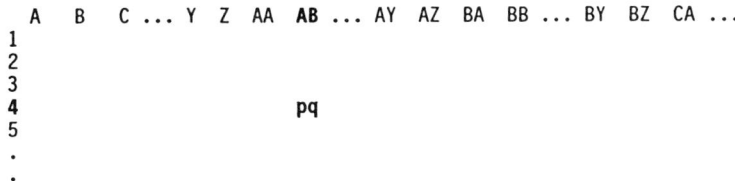

Figure 1. Spreadsheet cell references

Text in spreadsheets

Although spreadsheets are primarily designed to manipulate arithmetical data, as mentioned in the previous section they do provide for the entry of text. When text is inserted into a spreadsheet, it is described as a label. The label can automatically be centred, left- or right- adjusted *within its cell* as the user indicates, and the choice may be varied from cell to cell. If left-adjustment is adopted, a further characteristic of spreadsheet programs can be used to advantage in laying out pedigrees. To understand this key feature for pedigree work, it is necessary to give a little more detail of basic spreadsheet structure.

Each *column* in a spreadsheet can accommodate a fixed number of text characters per line, the number being fixed by the user, and not necessarily the same for each column. Obviously every cell in a given column has the same width in character terms. The default column width is usually 8 or 9 characters. Suppose it is 9 and that a 25 character, left-adjusted label "bap 12 Apr 1833 at Marton" is entered into a cell. (Note that spaces *within the label* are counted, and that although this entry contains figures, it is purely a text entry. This would still be true even if the cell contained only the year thus: "1833". No arithmetic can be performed on text, but then this facility is not needed for pedigree work).

With a cell width of only 9 characters, you might expect the label mentioned above would be curtailed to either the first or last 9 characters: "bap 12 Ap" or "at Marton". In fact, if the cell *immediately to the right* of the one containing the entry has a label or any other entry in it, then the label just entered will indeed be restricted to the first 9 characters "bap 12 Ap".

The suppressed text is not corrupted or lost, it is merely concealed. The same principle applies to the next but one cell to the right of the one containing the label. If that were empty, then the residue of the label, after suppressing characters 10 - 18 of the entered label would be displayed: " Marton ". You've guessed it: if the entry in the intervening cell were then deleted, what would then be displayed, left adjusted, in the nominal 9 character cell into which it was entered would be the 25 characters: "bap 12 Apr 1833 at Marton"!

With this facility to display more characters than the cell itself can contain, providing the next or sufficient cells to the right are empty, we can standardise on a narrow column width to provide the maximum of flexibility in positioning entries across a page. (Note that an **empty** cell contains very precisely nothing at all. A 9 character entry of spaces "   " is NOT nothing, even though nothing is displayed on screen or on paper).

To illustrate the advantage of a narrow column width, if we choose a standard column width of 15 to accommodate the minimum basic entry such as "bap 12 Apr 1833" we are restricted to only 6 columns per page on an A4 layout at 12 characters per inch, allowing for reasonable margins. However, the minimum spacing between individuals would then also be 15 characters (one column width), whereas 3 characters would adequately separate them. The effect of this large, standard column width would thus reduce the page capacity to 3 individuals across the page.

However, if a column width of only 3 characters is chosen, an A4 page-width can at a pinch contain an improved total of 4 individuals, each sibling requiring 5 columns to accommodate an entry, with 1 blank column between individuals. This is still too small a number to be practical however, and further ways of increasing the number of individuals per page width are necessary. It should be noted though that the standard 3 character width also provides the minimum space for the usual marriage indicator of " = " so this cell size is the obvious standard unit, 15 characters for a "bap", "mar" or "bur" entry requiring 5 standard units with no wasted space.

More people per page

The problem of increasing the number of individuals per page width can be tackled in two ways. One is to use A3 paper, which requires a wide carriage printer. The other, open to most computerised genealogists, is to use a compressed typeface which crams in more than the 12 characters per inch of standard elite type. This compressed printing is possible with dot-matrix, ink-jet and laser printers.

The compression is achievable because spreadsheet programs have the facility to send special codes to the printer which control the number of characters per inch that are printed. If a code to print at 20 characters per inch is embedded at the top of the spreadsheet page, with a corresponding code to return the printer to its normal character spacing entered in the last line of the spreadsheet, we can print our pedigrees much more compactly without interfering with other uses of the printer. This is easily done, although it is more esoteric than simple text entry of course. The result is that A4 pages can then hold data for 8 individuals across the page and still leave reasonable margins.

Realise that this is 8 individuals and not necessarily 8 siblings. It might be 6 siblings and the spouses of two who married. It is a practical proposition for pedigrees however, although combination with the use of A3 paper produces the much better capacity of 12 individuals per page width.

In a similar way to controlling the number of characters per line, the spreadsheet can contain printer control codes to increase the number of lines per inch from the standard value of 6. In practice, combined with 20 characters per inch horizontal spacing, 8 lines per inch vertically is the maximum that can be used while ensuring legibility. On A4 paper, allowing space for headings and top and bottom margins dictated by the mechanics of the printer, about 60 - 65 lines of pedigree can be accommodated. Since each individual takes up typically 12 or 13 lines after allowing for the genealogical connecting lines, this means that the depth capacity of an A4 page is 5 individuals. A3 paper increases this to 7 individuals.

It is obvious from all this that use of A3 paper is to be desired. Its capacity is better suited to genealogical needs, and the ensuing legibility is such that once the final A3 master pedigree page is produced, even with a 9-pin dot-matrix printer, photocopier reduction to A4 size gives a clear yet compact page of pedigree. However, an A4 size original can be used, but a given pedigree will obviously then extend over more pages with the resulting need for more connector boxes, so that the pedigree is not so readily comprehensible. However, even an A4 version produced and printed using a spreadsheet program is clearer - and often neater! - than a hand-drawn pedigree, and additionally, it is possible to correct the spreadsheet version with speed and ease. How many painstakingly scripted pedigrees do you have awaiting redrafting to incorporate the result of more recent research?

Cursor movement macros

Movement of the cursor about the spreadsheet is normally by line or column, although full screen width or depth movement can also be effected. Pedigree work in a spreadsheet however requires convenient horizontal movement somewhere between these limits. It therefore makes sense to use another standard spreadsheet facility: macros. A macro is a sequence of spreadsheet program commands to which the user gives a unique reference "name". For speed and simplicity of use, this name is best restricted to a single letter. By judicious choice of letter, the "name" of the macro can be mnemonic, as in the examples which follow.

Each macro is recorded in an area of the spreadsheet which is not used as a working area, nor included in that part of the spreadsheet which will be printed out. Then, instead of having manually to repeat that same sequence of commands each time the action for which the macro is designed is required, all that is necessary is to invoke the macro using its "name". In the case of Lotus 1-2-3 and its clones, that means simultaneously pressing the <alt> key and the appropriate letter . The spreadsheet program then runs through the recorded commands automatically.

These commands can include movement to left or right a stated number of columns, movement up or down a stated number of rows, copying the contents of a designated cell into the cell currently occupied by the cursor, and so on. Possible macros for pedigree work are obvious.

With 3-character width columns in the pedigree part of the spreadsheet, a standard 5 column width for data entry (which thus defines a standard block width of 15 characters for a given individual) and a *minimum* space of one column between individuals, successive individuals appear at 6 column intervals at a minimum, so a macro named "r" to move 6 columns to the right is obviously going to be useful. The sequence of Lotus 1-2-3 commands which make up this macro, and for all the macros which are described later in this booklet, are given in Appendix A.

Marriage indicator macros

Another useful macro is one that moves 5 columns to the right, inserts " = " in the cell the cursor has just reached before moving one further cell to the right in readiness for entering details of the spouse. Since the action of this macro goes "one step beyond" that of macro "r", its mnemonic name is "s" - "one step beyond" r alphabetically, or alternatively "s" for "spouse". A closely related macro is one which omits the initial 5 column rightwards movement, merely placing " = " in the present cursor position before moving right one cell. The obvious mnemonic name for this macro is "m" (for "married to"). Similar is one for use in linking the parents of an illegitimate child making use of the tilde sign " ≈ ". Unsurprisingly, this macro is named "i"!

Family name macro

With the suggested 15 character width for the data block for each individual, forename(s) and surname need to appear on successive lines. On each spreadsheet therefore, it is useful to enter the family surname in a cell in a standard position in the macro recording area. Such a macro ("n", for "name"), when invoked, copies the contents of the family name cell into the one currently occupied by the cursor, then moves the cursor down 2 cells in readiness for entry of that individual's personal details. Thus it is only necessary to type in the family name once rather than perhaps 30 times on an A3 page.

A refinement to this family name macro is to insert a number of leading spaces before the surname so that the surname is centred over the 15-character data block for that individual, while retaining the same column for all entries in that individual's data block. To achieve this, add leading spaces as shown in Table 1.

Table 1

Number of letters in name	Number of leading spaces
3 or 4	6
5 or 6	5
7 or 8	4
9 or 10	3
11 or 12	2
13 or 14	1

The same number of leading spaces must then, of course, also be used before the forename(s) on the line above if the names are to align on the leftmost character. Alternatively, the table above can be used to centre the Christian name over the data block. By ensuring that ALL the entries in the individual's data block start in the same column, repositioning the block requires only the necessary rows in that single column to be moved en masse. Even though the number of characters in each row of the block exceeds the standard column width of 3 characters, nothing will be left behind!

Place name macros

A number of macros could be used to preset several place names such as " at Marton" or " at Gawsworth" which enter the parish name in the cell below the date in baptismal and burial entries, to save a lot of repetitive keying. Since the place names however vary from pedigree to pedigree, these macros would have to have name letters allocated to them arbitrarily (although if only one place name macro is used, it could be named "w" for "whereabouts" or even "d" for "designation", neither of which is *entirely* arbitrary!). Because of this variability of place name in different spreadsheets and the arbitrary macro naming if more than one place name is required, there is a better but more complex macro solution which is described later in the section "Menu macro of place names" (page 15), after the basic system has been fully explained.

Printer control macros

The pedigree spreadsheet should also have two printer control macros. Both set out the area of the total spreadsheet which is to be printed out. One instructs the printer to do this in draft mode ("p", for "proof quality"), while the other uses the slower letter quality print mode ("o", for "output quality").

Line drawing macros

Finally, and most importantly, there is a set of line drawing macros. One inserts a horizontal line across the whole cell. This is given the mnemonic name "h". Another ("v") places a vertical line in the centre character position of the cell. The remaining nine macros produce all the possible intersections of a horizontal and vertical line that can be needed in a 3 character cell. The nine possibilities together with their names are illustrated in Figure 2. Mnemonic naming for these is not as direct as for the horizontal and vertical lines, but is nevertheless logical and most importantly, easy to remember.

```
    a            b            c
    ┌            ┬            ┐

    j            k            l
    ├            ┼            ┤

    x            y            z
    └            ┴            ┘
```

Figure 2.   The single-line graphics

As shown in Figure 2, the nine possible intersections, if placed in adjacent cells, would form a square divided into quarters. This mental image can be used to give a mnemonic pattern to the relevant macro names. The top row of three intersections are named with the first three letters of the alphabet (the "top" of the alphabet), while the bottom row of three are named with the final three letters (the "bottom") of the alphabet. In each case the alphabetic sequence is used naturally from left to right. The middle row is slightly more obscure, but does use 3 consecutive letters from the "middle" of the alphabet. "k", a letter which for mnemonic purposes can be regarded as formed from four straight lines meeting at a point, is used to name the similarly formed central intersection. The alphabetic sequence of mnemonic macro names "j, k, l" for this row then naturally follows.

Although these line intersection macros use sophisticated commands to produce their symbols, and are more complex than the macros described so far, you only have to get them right once, so it is worth the effort! Note particularly that all these macros produce continuous lines, in contrast to the interrupted horizontal ("---") or vertical (" | ") lines normally produced by word processors. This results in the production, with ease, of a very professional looking, drop-line pedigree.

If it is wished to emphasise a line of descent by using double lines, say that of the male line leading to a particular individual, additional macros are required. These are described in the section headed "Menu macro of double-line graphics" on page 15, since they are not an essential feature of the basic system for using a spreadsheet program for pedigree work. Figure 3 opposite shows an extract from a pedigree produced by the basic method described here.

Headings and cross references

In order to provide a unique reference for each sheet of pedigree, each page should show the family name as a heading, and should be numbered in the style "Page 3 of 5" etc so that where continuation of a descent occurs, the continuation box can quote the continuation page and a unique identifying letter. Similarly the continuation box on the continuation page can display the same letter and the number of the earlier page on which the link is to be found. This is particularly useful if in recording collateral lines in the pedigree you endeavour to present the branches in parallel, since this results in each continuation usually being several pages further on. The alternative is to follow a line on successive pages before picking up for continuation an earlier branch. This method however separates by several pages individuals who are contemporaneous, such as cousins. A recommended style and layout for these headings, which produces a block which prints out in the top right hand corner of the pedigree, is described on page 14 with the necessary details given in Appendix B.

At the bottom left hand corner of the page, it is worth entering a "filename" in unobtrusive fine print. This "filename" is in reality the DOS file name of that particular spreadsheet, which is useful when it becomes necessary to recall a spreadsheet from perhaps 40 or 50 pedigree sheets to carry out additions or amendments. Details of how to achieve this "filename" insertion are also included in Appendix B.

Saving hard disk space

Since a typical A3 size spreadsheet is about 65-70 Kb in size, if hard disk capacity is limited, it is best not to retain the files permanently on the hard disk. Instead, retain a sub-directory within the spreadsheet program directory for holding pedigrees when required. This sub-directory should permanently contain a small batch file which loads the whole contents of a floppy disk into that pedigree sub-directory.

Your pedigrees should reside on a series of high density floppy disks, each of which covers several families. Each floppy disk in its turn contains a batch file which on exiting from the spreadsheet program, copies all the files back from the pedigree sub-directory to the floppy disk, thus archiving any changes or newly created pedigrees, then deletes the spreadsheet files from the hard disk. This is quick and convenient. Suitable batch files for this method of working are given in Appendix C.

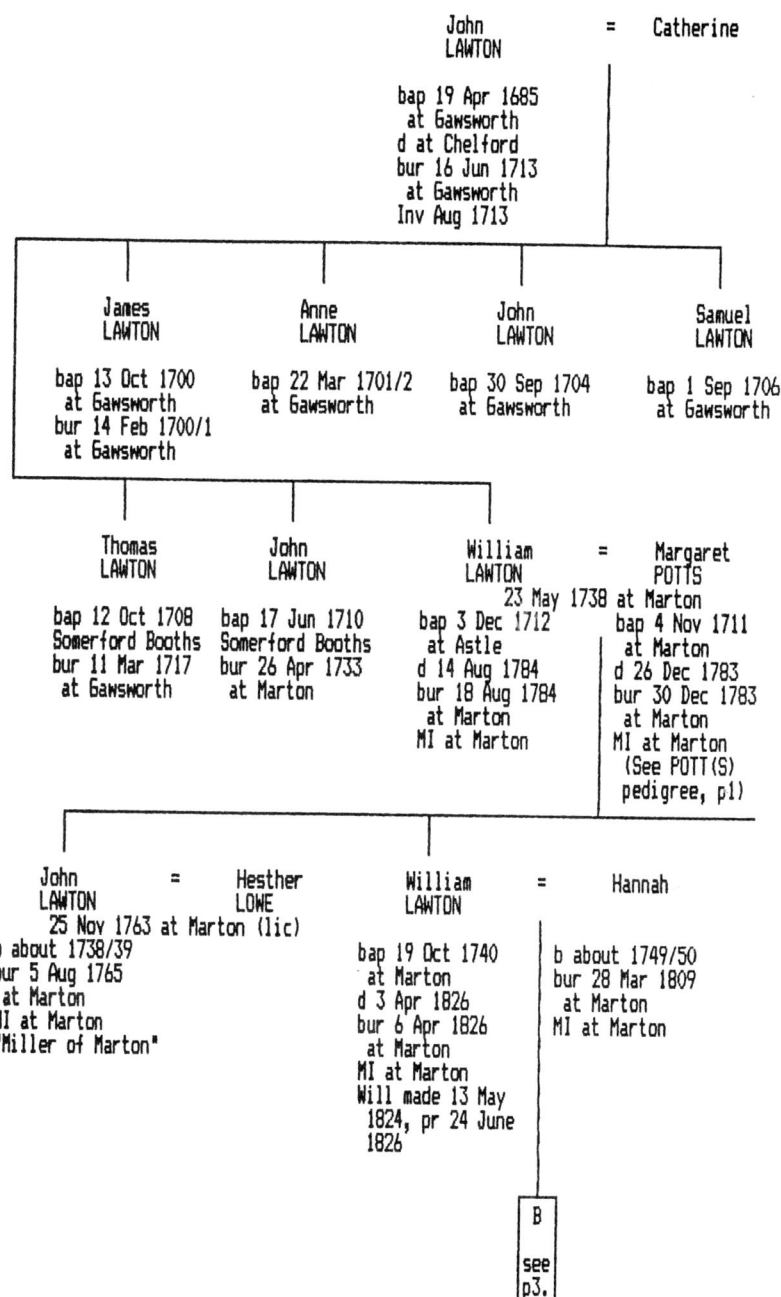

Figure 3. Pedigree extract using single-line graphics - the Lawton family in Cheshire

Master spreadsheet and new trees

The 21 macros described in this booklet should be held on a master spreadsheet which also contains standard *dummy* headings and the necessary printer control codes (as described in Appendix B) in the print out area to produce the different size and line pitch printing required. Whenever you start on a new family name you should load up a **copy** of this master spreadsheet, personalise the dummy name heading with the new family name, insert the surname in the family name cell in the macro area and save this revised spreadsheet as the family master spreadsheet. Successive pages of the pedigree are then created from a copy of this family master, remembering to alter as appropriate the dummy page/date heading.

It is helpful to rough out on a piece of scrap paper who will go where on the printed page before starting to key in data. Fine tuning of the positioning can be done when entry of the page data has been completed, since the amount of information for each individual is quite variable. The use of columns 3 characters wide facilitates this and an overall balanced effect is easily achieved.

ENHANCEMENTS TO THE BASIC SYSTEM

More layout details

Having given the details of the basic system for spreadsheet family trees it is now time to describe the refinements to the basic system alluded to in several of the preceding sections. Additionally some further detail of the layout of the pedigree worksheet will be described. To make matters clearer, the description will be of a recommended worksheet layout for A3 size pedigrees with any modification for an A4 size pedigree given in brackets.

As explained in the section "Text in spreadsheets" (page 5), the column widths in a spreadsheet (the number of characters each cell in a column *nominally* contains) do not all need to be the same. On the pedigree worksheet used for illustration in the rest of this booklet, column A has been set at 31 characters, column B at 42 characters and column C at 3 characters, giving a total of 76 characters. The significance of this total is that allowing for the permanent row number display, these 3 columns just fill the 80-character width of a standard computer display screen. Using the standard spreadsheet program facility to move left or right by exactly 1 screen width, means that from the Home cell it is possible to move directly to the top of the leftmost column of the pedigree worksheet, that is, to cell D1.

The widths of each of these first 3 columns is not critical, although clearly their total of 76 characters is, and you may vary them to suit your needs. Each cell in column C however should always contain the broken vertical line character | in its rightmost character position to serve as a visual warning during construction and maintenance of a page of pedigree of its left hand limit. These first 3 columns are not printed out, so the demarcation line in column C does not appear on the printed pedigree!

Location of macros

Columns A and B, rows 9 to 90 inclusive are used to hold most of the macros suggested in this booklet, the exceptions being the menu macros still to be described. The macros may be in any convenient order: alphabetical or grouped by type for instance. Column A shows the macro name (with the back-slash indicating the Alt key). If you wish, you may follow the macro name **with at least 1 space**, in turn followed by a brief description of the macro's function eg "\h Horizontal line". Take care that any description you do enter does NOT extend into column B. With the suggested width of column A of 31 characters, a maximum of 28 characters are thus available for the description.

Alongside the name, enter in column B the first (and usually only) instruction contained in the corresponding macro command, with any required further instructions in that same macro in the column B cell(s) immediately below. The cell in column B following the final instruction in the macro **must always be** an empty one, to signal to the spreadsheet program the end of the sequence of instructions included in that macro. It follows that the spacing of the macro descriptions in column A is irregular, but because all the information on the macros is contained in the width of the screen, "paging" up or down a screenfull at a time (usually 20 rows) makes it easy to find, check, and if necessary edit the repertoire of macros. An example of this macro layout is given in Figure 4.

```
           A                      B                          C
22
23      \h              /cA84~~
24
25      \i              ≈ {RIGHT}~
26
27      \j              ├~
28
29      \k              /cA87~~
30
31      \l              /cA88~~
32
33      \m              ={RIGHT}~
34
35      \n              name
36                      {DOWN 2}~
37
38      \o              /PPRD1..BU117~G{ESC 2}
38
40      \p              /PPRD2..BU117~G{ESC 2}
41
```

Figure 4. Screen layout of macro names and macros.

Above row 9, columns A and B are used for a description of the special uses of the first 9 lines of the pedigree worksheet itself. Similar use occurs in columns A and B opposite the final 2 rows of the pedigree printout area. Details are given in Appendix B, and it should be noted that in that Appendix and also in Appendix A, because the spacing is important, * is used to represent the entry in the worksheet **NOT of an asterisk itself but of a single space character**. Be careful to remember this convention when entering the key sequences from Appendixes A and B into the spreadsheet.

Page limits

In the descriptions below and in Appendix B, cell references apply to both A4 and A3 size worksheets *unless* the reference is followed by a different reference in curly brackets. Should this occur, the initial cell reference relates to A3 size worksheets, the curly bracket reference to A4 size worksheets.

Columns D to BV {AZ} inclusive are each 3 characters wide. Each cell in column BV {AZ} contains the vertical line character | (a broken line on most keyboards) in its leftmost character position to mark the right hand limit of the pedigree entry area. This complements the left hand limit in column C, mentioned on page 12. These columns are not printed out, neither is row 118 {80} which indicates the foot of the pedigree page by containing a horizontal line. The rectangle of information to be printed out therefore runs from cell D1 (output quality) or cell D2 (proof quality, which is quicker to print) to the diagonally opposite corner at cell BU117 {AY79}. Since the first eight and the last two rows are used for printer control and standard entries, **the area available for actual pedigree entry is from cell D9 to cell BU115 {AY77}**.

Title block

The positioning and spacing given in Appendix B of the dummy entries in cells AC4 {Q4} and BE7 {AG7} is important. This is because the printing of "name PEDIGREE" in double size starting in cell AC4 {Q4}, whilst the page number and date are in condensed elite typeface starting in cell BE7 {AG7}, with a blank line in row 6, will result in a neatly aligned block in the top right-hand corner of the printout as shown in Figure 5. When therefore the actual family name contains more than 4 letters, for every TWO extra letters, start the entry ONE character to the left of the n of "name". This may necessitate moving the entry one or even two cells to the left and adjusting the number of leading spaces as appropriate. Final fine tweaking of the block can be done by varying the leading spaces before "Page" and/or between the end of the page number and start of the date. The suggested start cells and spacing provide a good first-pass fit however.

LAWTON PEDIGREE
Page 1 of 8   26 Oct 1989

Figure 5. Pedigree title block

Location of menu macros

Rows 120 to 143, starting in column D, contain 2 further macros. The reason for placing these macros apart from the others is because one of them does, and one may, contain entries which significantly exceed the width of column B. Placing them **below** the pedigree entry area avoids any risk of user-entries spilling over into the pedigree print area.

Menu macro of place names

It was stated in the section "Place name macros" (page 8) that while it is possible to use a number of arbitrarily named place name macros, it is difficult to remember which macro name enters which place name, since the place names vary in different pedigrees. It is therefore more convenient to replace several place name macros with a single one, named "**w**" as suggested on page 8, which presents a *menu* of place names. This macro by the way concludes with an instruction to move the cursor down 1 row after making the entry. Such movement is usually required and so is worth including in the macro.

The menu options are customized for the individual page of the pedigree in which they appear, and there can be from 1 to 8 possibilities, which is more than ample. Since the place name descriptions which the menu *displays on screen* do not have to match exactly the place name which will be *entered into the pedigree*, it is generally easy to arrange that each name *in the menu* starts with a different letter. This ensures that the menu selection can be made merely by entering the first letter of the menu name. This is simpler and quicker than moving the cursor with the arrow keys and then pressing the enter key. However, moving the cursor over a menu name results in the full entry appropriate to that selection being displayed on screen, so if you forget what the abbreviation indicated, all is not lost!

Menu macro of double-line graphics

The menu system utilised for place names is also suitable for adding an *additional* series of 15 line-intersection "graphics" to enable a completed pedigree to be embellished as suggested earlier by picking out a particular descent with double lines rather than single ones. Not all the theoretically possible intersection "graphics" of single and double lines can occur in a pedigree. For example, neither a vertical single line nor a vertical double line can join from above the middle of a double horizontal line. On the other hand, a descending vertical double line can turn left or right as a double line, with or without a single line in the opposite direction. There are also a very few possible single and double line intersections which cannot be constructed since the ASCII codes needed to form them do not exist. The only problem this presents is as an occasional design constraint to avoid such intersections when laying out the pedigree.

The required and achievable double line "graphics" fall into 2 groups. First there are 8 simple ones, which comprise:

(a) the intersections required for the top and bottom of connector boxes, the boxes always being made up from single lines. The menu names for these are "**o**" (or "**overbox**" if preferred) and "**u**" (or "**underbox**") respectively.

(b) the wholly double line intersections. These can be given as *menu* names the one letter *macro* names of their single line equivalents "**h**", "**v**", "**a**", "**c**", "**x**" and "**y**" for ease of recollection.

(The next two pages are a reduction from an A3 spreadsheet tree, the Luke family of Devon; the text continues on page 18.)

Pages 16 and 17. The Luke family of Devon, reduced from an A3 spreadsheet tree.

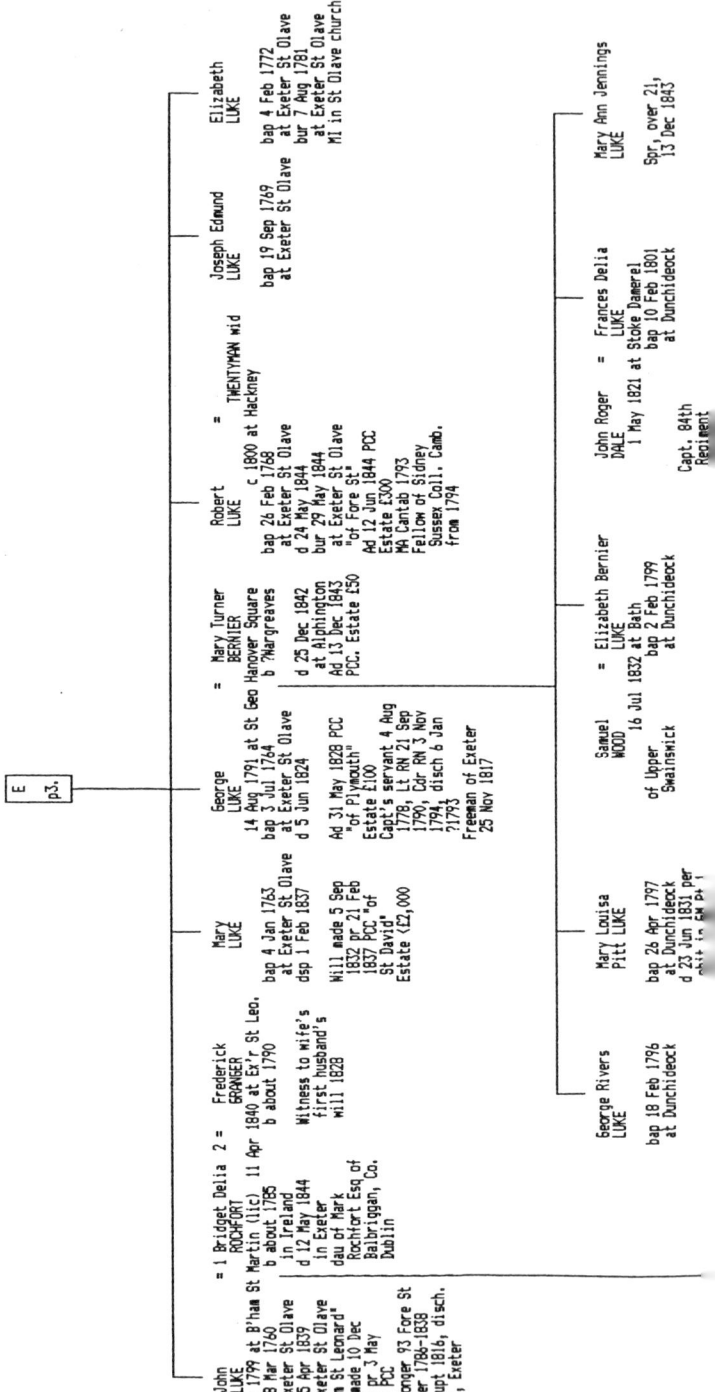

LUKE PEDIGREE

Page 4 of 6   18 Jul 1992

LUKE Family Tree

Generation 1 (Parents)

John Rochfort LUKE = **Ann Greaves SMITH** (lic)
- 26 Apr 1835 at Exeter St Thomas (lic)
- bap 15 Feb 1804 at Exeter St Olave
- d 6 Feb 1886
- bur 11 Feb 1886 at West Norwood
- Will made 8 & 28 Nov 1878 pr 8 Mar 1886 PPR
- Ironmonger with bro Geo, 93 Fore St Exeter 1837-47
- b 1806/07 at Barnwell, Leics.
- bur 22 Nov 1872 at West Norwood

George Carwithen LUKE = **Catherine COX wid nee CROSS**
- 3 Jun 1835 at Heavitree (lic)
- bap 13 Feb 1806 at Exeter St Olave
- Ironmonger with bro Jn, 93 Fore St Exeter 1837-47
- In Jersey Oct 1861
- eldest d of Henry Cross Esq
- Alive Oct 1861
- (Catherine Laura LUKE wid of Jersey alive Sep 1898 - ? the same person)

James Marwick LUKE
- bap 27 Dec 1807 at Exeter St Olave

Ann LUKE
- bap 19 Feb 1810 at Exeter St Olave
- bur 8 Aug 1839 at Exeter St Olave

Mary Delia LUKE
- bap 17 Nov 1811 at Exeter St Olave
- bur 19 Jan 1837 at Exeter St Olave

Frances Maria LUKE
- bap 14 Mar 1813 at Exeter St Olave
- Alive 30 Aug 1839

Children of John Rochfort LUKE & Ann Greaves SMITH

Eliza Rochfort LUKE
- bap 17 Dec 1801 at Exeter St Olave
- bur 26 Oct 1902 at Exeter St Olave

see pg.

Children of George Carwithen LUKE & Catherine

Bertha Carwithen LUKE
- bap 17 May 1838 at Topsham

Second Family Group

Frederick Augustus LUKE
- b 8 Jan 1815
- bap 11 Feb 1815 at Exeter St Olave
- dsp 1844
- In Philadelphia Aug 1839
- Ad 17 Jun 1844 Estate £1,000

Charles LUKE
- b 1 Aug 1818
- bap 6 Sep 1818 at Exeter St Olave
- In Philadelphia Aug 1839

Mark Rochfort LUKE
- b 3 Apr 1820
- bap 19 Mar 1821 at Exeter St Olave

Richard Rochfort LUKE
- b 14 Jun 1821
- bap 1 Aug 1821 at Exeter St Olave
- Alive Oct 1861
- d by Dec 1907

= **William MUNK MD**
- b 24 Sep 1816 at Battle
- d 20 Dec 1898 at Finsbury Sq London
- c 1849 in Exeter

Emma LUKE
- b 15 May 1823
- bap 12 Jun 1823 at Exeter St Olave

Next Generation

Gerald Rochfort LUKE = **Winifred WALTERS**
- 11 Dec 1907 Rochford (Essex) Registry Office
- b 1867/8
- b 1884/5

Issue 2s, 3d

PLUK:04

These simple "graphics" with their unique but mnemonic menu names are shown in Figure 6.

```
    overbox      underbox        h           v
      ⊥⊥           ⊤⊤           ══          ‖‖

      a             c            x           z
      ┌═           ═┐           └═          ═┘
```

Figure 6. The "easy" double-line graphics

The remaining 7 more complex intersections all contain both single and double lines. For 3 of them it is possible to use as *menu* names the one letter *macro* names of their wholly single line equivalents, which makes these unique within this menu and also different from the earlier menu names as well.

In order to provide for the remaining 4 "graphics", menu names which have totally unique first letters, it is necessary to start them with the otherwise unused, arbitrary consecutive first letters d, e, f and g. In each case this is followed by the underline sign to help the eye pick out the following 2 letters, which are the significant ones. Although the order is variable, these are h (for horizontal) and one of the standard "corner" names a, c, x and y. The left to right order of these 2 significant letters following the underline sign is the same as the left to right order of occurrence in the relevant "graphic" of the single line horizontal and the double line corner. Not very good nor easy to describe but the best that can be managed to achieve unique single letter menu names for these final 4 "graphics". These 7 more complex "graphics" and their menu names are shown in Figure 7.

```
    d_ha         e_hx         f_ch         g_zh
    ┬┌═          ┴└═          ═┐┬          ═┘┴

     b                         j             l
    ═┬═                       ‖├            ┤‖
```

Figure 7. The single-line/double-line intersection graphics

These menu macros make use of the so-called /X Macro Command M. The original Lotus 1-2-3 version set a limit of 8 selections within a menu, but some of the 1-2-3 clones have raised this limit. In this case it may be possible to put all 15 of these double-line macros into a single menu, and with the menu names suggested above there is no duplication of initial letters of the menu names to prevent this being done.

Incidentally, the menu names which appear across the screen when the macro is invoked, do not have to be in alphabetical order. As already mentioned, when the cursor is moved along this list of names, the effect of the highlighted name is displayed on the line below the menu names, so if you forget what a particular menu name means, you can see the corresponding "graphic" before you select it. It therefore makes sense to put the 4 awkward ones like d_ha at the left of the menu list to speed selection for preview purposes.

The single menu macro (or if forced, each of the two menu macros) described above for printing double lines where required need(s) to be given a single letter macro name. If only a single menu macro is used, "d" for "double line graphics" is obvious. However, if 2 menu macros are created, since the unused letters are now few in number, selecting unique letters which are also mnemonic requires some lateral thinking! In this case, "e" for "easy" is suggested for the 8 simple intersections, with "f", the next letter in the alphabet for the associated more complex graphics macro.

Figure 8 reproduces the same pedigree extract given earlier in Figure 3, this time with the double line macros used to pick out the main descent. The comparison may help you to decide if you wish to add this graphics menu facility to your spreadsheet pedigrees.

Autostart macro for initial cursor position

Whilst on the subject of macros, if the facility is available, you can use an autostart macro (alt-0 in Lotus 1-2-3) so that the spreadsheet program automatically places the cursor in the top left hand corner of the pedigree entry area (cell D9) when the worksheet is retrieved. The macro to achieve this is included in Appendix A.

Cross-references to husband's trees

One other point. Although not essential, it is consistent to place the **husband**'s details to the left of those of his spouse in all cases. This will present no layout problem even when the relevant page of the pedigree gives the ancestry of his wife, since his data block can merely cross reference the name of the pedigree (and page if necessary) where *his* ancestry is to be found, so no connector box needs to appear above his name.

Positioning marriage details

Finally, on the line beneath the surnames, enter the couple's marriage details in the same column as the other entries in the **husband**'s data block (or the data block of the **wife** if this appears to the left of her spouse's). This entry should be in the style "<date> at <place name>". The date should be in the form dd mmm yyyy for example "6 Jul 1776 at Mary Tavy". To centre details given in this format below the marriage ("equals") sign requires the insertion of leading spaces as shown in Table 2.

Table 2

Number of letters in place name	Number of leading spaces
5 or 6	5
7 or 8	4
9 or 10	3
11 or 12	2
13 or 14	1

Clearly, if the surname in the first spouse's data block exceeds 15 characters, then that data block will need to exceed 5 cells in width, so that the table given above will not apply.

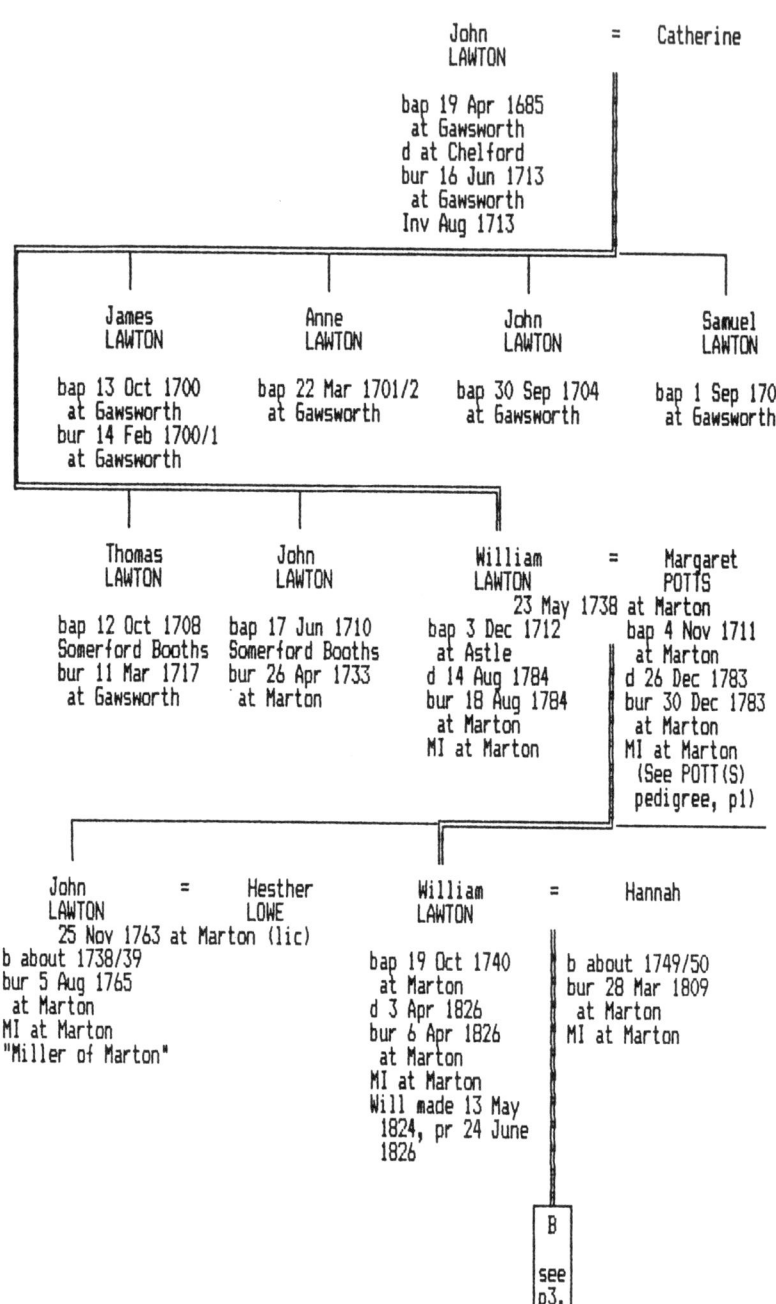

Figure 8. Pedigree extract using double-line graphics

Appendix A   **Pedigree worksheet macros**

Lotus 1-2-3 macros using the names given in the text of this booklet are detailed below. Because the spacing is important, in listing the macro instructions below, * is used to represent the entry in the worksheet **NOT of an asterisk itself but of a single space character**. Be careful to remember this convention when entering the key strokes into the spreadsheet. Quotation marks should be keyed in as shown, as should the tilde sign ~ which is used in Lotus 1-2-3 macros to represent the <ENTER> key. Note that there are sometimes 2 successive tilde signs to be entered.

It is also important to note that a number of macros involve the *copying* of the contents of a cell which holds a graphic of a line intersection. This is because the graphic in the referenced cell does **NOT** contain a space in the first character position of the 3 character wide cell. Failure to operate the macro by copying may cause errors.

In the case of those macros that draw any sort of graphic, for clarity the macro details given below are in several parts. These parts include the precise character string to produce the graphic which should be entered into the cell which is to hold the graphic. The location for this cell is given following the name of the macro or menu item as the case may be.

A description such as "1st cell [B9]" means enter the string in the first cell of the macro where the choice of that cell is left to the user, or in cell B9 if the layout of the worksheet suggested in this booklet is used. These references in square brackets apply to both A3 and A4 size worksheets. For more complex cases a specific location only is quoted, again applicable to both A3 and A4 size worksheets. This specific location is then used as the source cell for the copy instruction in the macro itself. The location may be changed as desired, but take care to ensure that any change in the cell used to hold the graphic is correspondingly changed elsewhere in the macro.

Having entered the character string for the graphic, press <ENTER>: the string will convert into the graphic it generates in the cell into which the string was entered, although the string will still be displayed if the cell contents are examined, so it can still be edited. To make the graphic permanent invoke the Range Value command using the menu (or by typing /RV) and press <ENTER> twice.

If the cell contents are now examined the line intersection graphic will be seen, NOT the generating character string, which cannot now be edited. Because of this, it will save keying time when entering the macros if, **BEFORE INVOKING THE RANGE VALUE COMMAND**, cell copying is used to enter similar character strings for other macros, which can then be edited as required. Thus, for example, enter the character string for macro **a**, copy it for macros **j** and **x**, then for the latter, edit the numbers in the first @CHAR command from 218 to 195 and 192 respectively. To facilitate macro entry in this way, the macros have been grouped by type in the list which follows, and within each type macros with similar character strings follow one another for ease of input as just described.

For those macros where the required graphic is NOT obtained by copying from another location, eg macros **a**, **v**, etc, once the Range Value command has been invoked, the cell is edited to complete the macro by adding the tilde sign **immediately following** the graphic. Since the graphic may itself incorporate a space at the right hand end of the cell, do not be misled by the appearance of the "actual macro" below into adding a space before the tilde! Remember, if spaces are to be entered in these macros, an asterisk will be shown for each space character required. So no asterisk, no space! As an illustration, the 3 character wide graphic macro **v** is a central vertical line with a space either side so there is **no need to insert a space** between the graphic macro and the tilde sign.

Note that in the macro creation details which follow, no description of the function of the macro has been given. See the section "Location of macros" on page 12 should you wish to add this information. Using the suggested references throughout will result in the macros appearing in alphabetical order in column B, except for the special menu macros **d** and **w** which will appear below the pedigree layout area.

In the case of the menu macros for the double line graphics and the place names, although the locations given may be altered, it is suggested that the specific locations given are adhered to in the case of A3 size spreadsheets. If desired, in A4 sized spreadsheets the row numbers in each case may be decreased by 30 to bring them closer to the lower edge of the pedigree area.

The following alphabetical list of the macro names, indicating the sections where the macros are described may be helpful:

Macro	Section	Page
a, b, c	Line drawing macros	9
d	Menu macro of double-line graphics	15
h	Line drawing macros	9
i	Marriage indicator macros	8
j, k, l	Line drawing macros	9
m	Marriage indicator macros	8
n	Family name macro	8
o, p	Printer control macros	9
r	Cursor movement macros	7
s	Marriage indicator macros	8
v	Line drawing macros	9
w	Menu macro of place names	15
x, y, z	Line drawing macros	9
0 (zero)	Autostart macro for initial cursor position	19

1. **Single line macros**

Name: **a**   Location of character string: 1st cell [B9]
Character string:
@REPEAT("*",1)&@REPEAT(@CHAR(218),1)&@REPEAT(@CHAR(196),1)
Location of macro   1st cell [B9]   Actual macro: ┌~

Name: **j**   Location of character string: 1st cell [B27]
Character string:
@REPEAT("*",1)&@REPEAT(@CHAR(195),1)&@REPEAT(@CHAR(196),1)
Location of macro   1st cell [B27]   Actual macro: ├~

Name: **x**   Location of character string: 1st cell [B61]
Character string:
@REPEAT("*",1)&@REPEAT(@CHAR(192),1)&@REPEAT(@CHAR(196),1)
Location of macro   1st cell [B61]   Actual macro: └~

Name: **b**   Location of character string: A85
Character string:
@REPEAT(@CHAR(196),1)&@REPEAT(@CHAR(194),1)&@REPEAT(@CHAR(196),1)
Appearance of graphic in cell A85: ─┬─
Location of macro   B11   Actual macro: /cA85~~

Name: **k**   Location of character string: A87
Character string:
@REPEAT(@CHAR(196),1)&@REPEAT(@CHAR(197),1)&@REPEAT(@CHAR(196),1)
Appearance of graphic in cell A87: ─┼─
Location of macro   B29   Actual macro: /cA87~~

Name: **y**   Location of character string: A89
Character string:
@REPEAT(@CHAR(196),1)&@REPEAT(@CHAR(193),1)&@REPEAT(@CHAR(196),1)
Appearance of graphic in cell A89: ─┴─
Location of macro   B63   Actual macro: /cA89~~

Name: **c**   Location of character string: A86
Character string:
@REPEAT(@CHAR(196),1)&@REPEAT(@CHAR(191),1)&@REPEAT("*",1)
Appearance of graphic in cell A86: ─┐
Location of macro   B13   Actual macro: /cA86~~

<< where an asterisk * is shown in a character string type a space >>

(Single line macros, continued)

Name: l   Location of character string: A88

Character string:
@REPEAT(@CHAR(196),1)&@REPEAT(@CHAR(180),1)&@REPEAT("*",1)

Appearance of graphic in cell A88:   ⌐

Location of macro   B31   Actual macro: /cA88~~

Name: z   Location of character string: A90

Character string:
@REPEAT(@CHAR(196),1)&@REPEAT(@CHAR(217),1)&@REPEAT("*",1)

Appearance of graphic in cell A90:   ⌐

Location of macro   B65   Actual macro: /cA90~~

Name: h   Location of character string: A84

Character string:
@REPEAT(@CHAR(196),3)

Appearance of graphic in cell A84:   ──

Location of macro   B23   Actual macro: /cA84~~

Name: v   Location of character string: 1st cell [B52]

Character string:
@REPEAT("*",1)&@REPEAT(@CHAR(179),1)&@REPEAT("*",1)

Location of macro   1st cell [B52]   Actual macro: | ~

---

2. **Menu macros**

Double line graphics

Name: d   Location of menu generating macro: D124

Menu generating macro: /xmD120~

This menu macro requires the entry of the 15 distinct graphics character strings and their related display macros which follow. Changing the column letters from those given will merely alter the left-to-right order of the menu names which appear on screen, since this follows the alphabetic sequence of the columns. There must not be any gap in this alphabetic sequence ie the menu items must be in successive columns.

If the row numbers are changed, it is important that all the menu names appear on the same row, and that the rows used for the menu name, character string and the actual macro for a particular menu item are consecutive and in the order just stated.

<< where an asterisk * is shown in a character string type a space >>

Finally, whichever column holds the details for the leftmost on-screen menu name **must additionally hold a macro command like /xmAN~ where A is the column letter and N is the row number holding the menu name,** (D is substituted for A and 120 is substituted for N using the specific locations given here) **and this macro command must appear in the row immediately below the macro for that leftmost menu item.**

Note that where the display macro given below starts with an actual graphic, this is entered into the cell by copying the relevant character string AFTER it has been converted using the Range Value command as described at the start of this Appendix. The cell is then edited to add the tilde sign immediately following the graphic also as described at the start of this Appendix.

The 15 menu item macros follow:

Menu name: **d_ha**   Location of menu name: D120
Location of character string: D121
Character string:
@REPEAT(@CHAR(196),1)&@REPEAT(@CHAR(201),1)&@REPEAT(@CHAR(205),1)
Appearance of graphic in cell D121: ─╔═
Location of display macro: D122   Display macro: /cD121~~

Menu name: **e_hx**   Location of menu name: E120
Location of character string: E121
Character string:
@REPEAT(@CHAR(196),1)&@REPEAT(@CHAR(200),1)&@REPEAT(@CHAR(205),1)
Appearance of graphic in cell E121: ─╚═
Location of display macro: E122   Display macro: /cE121~~

Menu name: **f_ch**   Location of menu name: F120
Location of character string: F121
Character string:
@REPEAT(@CHAR(205),1)&@REPEAT(@CHAR(187),1)&@REPEAT(@CHAR(196),1)
Appearance of graphic in cell F121: ═╗─
Location of display macro: F122   Display macro: /cF121~~

Menu name: **g_zh**   Location of menu name: G120
Location of character string: G121
Character string:
@REPEAT(@CHAR(205),1)&@REPEAT(@CHAR(188),1)&@REPEAT(@CHAR(196),1)
Appearance of graphic in cell G121: ═╝─
Location of display macro: G122   Display macro: /cG121~~

<< where an asterisk * is shown in a character string type a space >>

(double line macros, continued)

Menu name: a   Location of menu name: H120
Location of character string: H121
Character string:
@REPEAT("*",1)&@REPEAT(@CHAR(201),1)&@REPEAT(@CHAR(205),1)
Appearance of graphic in cell H121:   ╔═
Location of display macro: H122   Display macro: ╔═~

Menu name: x   Location of menu name: M120
Location of character string: M121
Character string:
@REPEAT("*",1)&@REPEAT(@CHAR(200),1)&@REPEAT(@CHAR(205),1)
Appearance of graphic in cell M121:   ╚═
Location of display macro: M122   Display macro: ╚═~

Menu name: c   Location of menu name: J120
Location of character string: J121
Character string:
@REPEAT(@CHAR(205),1)&@REPEAT(@CHAR(187),1)&@REPEAT("*",1)
Appearance of graphic in cell J121:   ═╗
Location of display macro: J122   Display macro: /cJ121~~

Menu name: z   Location of menu name: N120
Location of character string: N121
Character string:
@REPEAT(@CHAR(205),1)&@REPEAT(@CHAR(188),1)&@REPEAT("*",1)
Appearance of graphic in cell N121:   ═╝
Location of display macro: N122   Display macro: /cN121~~

Menu name: h   Location of menu name: O120
Location of character string: O121
Character string:
@REPEAT(@CHAR(205),3)
Appearance of graphic in cell O121:   ═══
Location of display macro: O122   Display macro: /cO121~~

---

26   << where an asterisk * is shown in a character string type a space >>

(double line macros, continued)

Menu name: **b** Location of menu name: I120
Location of character string: I121
Character string:
@REPEAT(@CHAR(205),1)&@REPEAT(@CHAR(209),1)&@REPEAT(@CHAR(205),1)
Appearance of graphic in cell I121: ╤
Location of display macro: I122 Display macro: /cI121~~

Menu name: **v** Location of menu name: P120
Location of character string: P121
Character string:
@REPEAT("*",1)&@REPEAT(@CHAR(186),1)&@REPEAT("*",1)
Appearance of graphic in cell P121: ║
Location of display macro: P122 Display macro: ║ ~

Menu name: **j** Location of menu name: K120
Location of character string: K121
Character string:
@REPEAT("*",1)&@REPEAT(@CHAR(199),1)&@REPEAT(@CHAR(196,1)
Appearance of graphic in cell K121: ╟
Location of display macro: K122 Display macro: ╟~

Menu name: **l** Location of menu name: L120
Location of character string: L121
Character string:
@REPEAT(@CHAR(196,1)&@REPEAT(@CHAR(182),1)&@REPEAT("*",1)
Appearance of graphic in cell L121: ╢
Location of display macro: L122 Display macro: /cL121~~

Menu name: **o** Location of menu name: Q120
Location of character string: Q121
Character string:
@REPEAT(@CHAR(196,1)&@REPEAT(@CHAR(208),1)&@REPEAT(@CHAR(196),1)
Appearance of graphic in cell Q121: ╨
Location of display macro: Q122 Display macro: /cQ121~~

<< where an asterisk * is shown in a character string type a space >>

(double line macros, continued)

Menu name: **u**	Location of menu name:	R120
Location of character string: R121		
Character string: @REPEAT(@CHAR(196),1)&@REPEAT(@CHAR(210),1)&@REPEAT(@CHAR(196),1)		
Appearance of graphic in cell R121: ╥		
Location of display macro: R122	Display macro:	/cR121~~

- **Place name menu**

Name: **w**	Location of menu generating macro:	D135
Menu generating macro: /xmD130~		

This menu macro requires the entry of a number of place names and their related display macros as detailed below. The menu names should be any meaningful but unique abbreviation for the corresponding place names. The column which contains the menu generating macro (D in this case, but it may be changed as desired) **must be the leftmost column of the macro and place names etc MUST be in successive columns**.

In what follows "abbrev" and "placename" are user-selected abbreviations and place names required for a particular worksheet. The master worksheet should be constructed with 2 menu items only using dummy names such as those used below. Additional columns can then be added when needed by copying the 2nd menu item column as many times as required, before editing the dummy entries to particularise them.

The 1st menu item macro is as follows:

Menu name: **abbrev1**	Location of menu name:	D131
Location of place name 1:	D132	
Entry in D132:	*at*placename1	
Location of display macro: D133	Display macro:	~{DOWN}

The 2nd menu item macro is as follows:

Menu name: **abbrev2**	Location of menu name 2:	E131
Location of place name 2:	E132	
Entry in E132:	*at*placename2	
Location of display macro: E133	Display macro:	~{DOWN}

<< where an asterisk * is shown in a character string type a space >>

The subsequent menu item macros follow the same pattern, the column letter being advanced one alphabetically each time. **Note that only the 1st menu item column contains the menu generating macro.**

3. Printing macros

Name: o	Location of character string: 1st cell [B38]	
Character string:		
For A3 size paper	/PPRD1..BU117~G{ESC*2}	
For A4 size paper	/PPRD1..AY79~G{ESC*2}	

Name: p	Location of character string: 1st cell [B40]	
Character string:		
For A3 size paper	/PPRD2..BU117~G{ESC*2}	
For A4 size paper	/PPRD2..AY79~G{ESC*2}	

4. Other pedigree macros

Name: i   Location of character string: 1st cell [B25]
Character string:
@REPEAT("*",1)&@REPEAT(@CHAR(247),1)&@REPEAT("*",1)
Location of macro   1st cell [B25]   Actual macro: ≈ {RIGHT}~

Name: m   Location of character string: 1st cell [B33]
Location of macro   1st cell [B33]   Actual macro: *=*{RIGHT}~

Name: n   Location of character string: 1st cell [B35]
Location of macro   1st cell & one below [B35 & B36]
Actual macro: NAME   (NAME is a dummy as explained in
                {DOWN 2}~   the main text of this booklet.
                             {DOWN 2}~ is entered in the cell
                             immediately beneath that contain-
                             ing the name)

Name: r   Location of character string: 1st cell [B46]
Location of macro   1st cell [B46]   Actual macro: {RIGHT 6}~

Name: s   Location of character string: 1st cell [B48]
Location of macro   1st cell [B48]
Actual macro: {RIGHT 5}~*=*{RIGHT}~

<< where an asterisk * is shown in a character string type a space >>

5. **Autostart macro**

Name: 0 (zero)   Location of character string: 1st cell [B67]
Location of macro   1st cell [B67]
Actual macro: {GOTO}C120~{GOTO}D9~

Appendix B   Standard layout and printer control strings

As explained in the main text of this booklet, because the spacing is important, * is used below to represent the entry in the worksheet **NOT of an asterisk itself but of a single space character**. Be careful to remember this convention when entering the key sequences from this Appendix into the spreadsheet.

The cell references given below apply to both A4 and A3 size worksheets *unless* the reference is followed by a different reference in curly brackets. Should this occur, the initial cell reference relates to A3 size worksheets, the curly bracket reference to A4 size worksheets.

Row	Text in Column A	Related entries elsewhere
1	Switch ON boldface	Control string in cell D1:- ||\027G
2	Switch ON condensed elite, 12 lines per inch	Control string in cell D2:- ||\015\027M\0273\027
3	Switch ON double-size print	Control string in cell D3:- ||\027\104\001
4	Pedigree family name	Cell AC4 {Q4} contains:- **name*PEDIGREE
5	Switch OFF double-size print	Control string in cell D5:- ||\027\104\000
6	Leave blank for spacing	
7	Page number & date	Cell BE7 {AG7} contains:- **Page*n*of*n********dd*mmm*19yy
8	Leave blank for spacing	

<< where an asterisk * is shown in a character string type a space >>

Row	Text in Column A	Related entries elsewhere
116 {78}	Switch ON superscript; filename; switch OFF superscript	A single character string for all this in cell D116 {D78} (The filename is, for example something like **LAW213**, indicating **LAW**ton pedigree, version **2**, page **13**). There are no spaces separating the 2 control strings and the filename. So the single character string *for this example* would be (note that there is a single quote character **but no vertical** lines at the start):- '\027SOLAW213\027T
117 {79}	Restore printer default settings	Control string in cell D117 {D79}:- ||\027H\027F\027P\0272
118 {80}	Limit of pedigree area	Horizontal line made up of equals signs in columns D to BU {AY} inclusive

Appendix C   Batch files

Suitable DOS batch file commands to load from and save to floppy disks to economise on hard disk space are as follows. See "Saving hard disk space" on page 10 for an explanation.

It is assumed in both batch files that the floppy drive to be used is Drive A and that the hard disk is Drive C. It is also assumed that the directory on the hard disk holding the spreadsheet program is called SPREADS and that the sub-directory of SPREADS holding the pedigree worksheets is called PEDS. These names will need changing to those actually used, as will possibly the drive letters A and C.

Batch file LOADUP

This should be held in C:\SPREADS\PEDS. Do not of course include in the batch file the explanatory material given below in square brackets:-

```
@ECHO OFF
CD C:\SPREADS\PEDS
PAUSE              Insert pedigree disk into Drive A
@ECHO OFF
CLS
@ECHO ON
REM      >>>>      Leave disk in floppy drive ready        <<<<
REM      >>>>      for back up on exit from SPREADS        <<<<
@ECHO OFF
COPY A:\*.WKS C:
C:\SPREADS\progname
```

[progname in the previous line is the .COM or .EXE filename of your spreadsheet software i.e. the name that the manual instructs you to use to run the program]

A:
BACKUP.BAT

Batch file BACKUP

This should be held - suitably modified - on each family floppy disk. Do not of course include in the batch file the explanatory material given below in square brackets:-

```
COPY C:\SPREADS\PEDS\famname1.WKS A:
COPY C:\SPREADS\PEDS\famnameN.WKS A:
```

[A similar line is required for each famname to be held on a particular disk. Assuming a naming convention as suggested in this booklet (3 alphabetic characters followed by 3 numeric characters), and that the families held on a particular disk are LAWTON, LUKE, ROCHFORT and SMALLWOOD, The four DOS famnames required might be LAW???, LUK???, ROC??? and SMA???. The question marks are "wild cards" to ensure that ALL the DOS files beginning with the given 3 alphabetic characters are picked up. There must be a question mark for each numeric character used, which should be the same total for all famnames.]

```
DEL C:\SPREADS\PEDS\*.BAK
```

[The last line deletes any back up copies that the spreadsheet program may have made. If the extension used for back up files differs from .BAK then substitute accordingly.]

```
DIR A:*.WKS
```

[To display the directory to indicate how much unused space is now left on the floppy disk.]

```
PAUSE
```